The Work Is Plentiful but Positive Male Role Models Are Few

The work to change and restore the lives of our young men in our communities today has become over whelming. The need for Positive Male Role Models and Positive Fathers is needed more now than ever before. The work remains plentiful, and the importance of the Positive Male Role Model remains evident.

Dr. Christopher S. King

Copyright © 2024

All Rights Reserved

ISBN: 978-1-963919-71-4

Dedication

This book is dedicated to all the men who have stayed true to our identity as providers, protectors, and teachers. I want to take this time to thank you for all the time, effort, and sacrifices you have made to ensure that our boys grow into positive and productive men. There is plenty of work yet to be done in our homes and communities; I am so thankful to have you on the battlefield with me as we set out to restore and reclaim the identity of our future Kings. I SALUTE YOU!

In memory of my loving mother.

Barbara J. Smith King

Acknowledgment

I'd like to take this time to acknowledge my wife, Mrs. Tannual King, for always—and I mean always—having my back. She has supported and encouraged me from the very start of writing this book, and for that, I am truly thankful.

To my young adults (children): Chris Jr., Sierra, P'Laura, Arriq, Kyeasta, and Michael, thank you for all you do to make me proud. To my pride and joy, my grandchildren, thank you for keeping PaPa alert and active and giving me the motivation I needed as I set out to be an example for you.

Last but not least, to my dear mother, my everything, I cannot do it justice by trying to explain what you mean to me, nor can I explain what it means to have had you as a mother, pouring your soul into Stefan, Patrick, and me. I hope I've made you proud. I love you, and I love you all.

Contents

Dedication v

Acknowledgment vii

About the Author xi

Introduction xiii

History of the Ultimate Role Model 1

Male Role Model Accountability 5

Real Life Short Stories 12

Interviewer #1 17

Interviewer #2 20

Interviewer #3 23

Interviewer #4 25

A Hand to Guide Me 27

Better Dads, Stronger Sons 29

Research 39

Father Abandonment: 49

Conclusion 59

REFERENCE 61

About the Author

Dr. Christopher S. King is a graduate of the School of Discipleship Seminary, where he earned his Doctoral Degree in Theology. He is a 100% Disabled Army Veteran who served in Desert Storm. He is also a retired fireman with 20 years of experience. Dr. King made history by becoming the first African American to be certified as a Mississippi State Firefighter in the city of Hazlehurst, MS. He was also the first African American in the city's history to earn the rank of Captain.

Dr. King is an ordained elder who was licensed to preach the gospel in 2019. He is the founder and president of The Power of One Outreach Ministry, whose goal is to ensure that every family has the opportunity to experience God's love by supporting them with resources such as housing, clothing, counseling, financial support, and employment.

Additionally, Dr. King is the facilitator for Disciples Brotherhood, an organization based in Tylertown, MS. The organization mentors teens in both local and neighboring communities, mentors young men appointed through the Juvenile Court System, and holds open discussions with men seeking to improve their lives through Godly counsel and real conversations.

Introduction

This book puts a spotlight on the challenges that our communities are facing due to the lack of Positive Male Role Models stepping up to the plate in support of our boys. My motivation for writing this book stems from countless conversations I've had with other concerned men. Over the years, I have witnessed firsthand the decline in self-respect, self-esteem, motivation, respect for elders, and regard for human life among today's young men in comparison to those of the past.

Whether it be talk throughout the neighborhood, conversations among friends and families over a meal, or a quiet night at home alone watching the evening news, we are constantly being reminded that many of our young men are seemingly losing their way. My concern is that the men of the past, who saw the need to be Positive Male Role Models for young men and took their roles as heads of the house and community seriously are now few and far between.

These men who made it their business to stay in our business, men who were on a mission to keep as many of us in check, trained, and mentored, as possible now seems to be falling by the waist side leaving our boys misled, misguided, and misdirected.

I appreciate how Proverbs 22:6 explains it in the New International Version of the Bible: *"Start children off on the way they should go, and even when they are old, they will not turn from it."*

I have taken the time to hear directly from the source, as the older folk used to say, praying and listening to God, interviewing men, women, and young people in our community in hopes of breaking down the barrier between our men and our youth. I have also found trustworthy and reliable resources through books and others sources to support my belief that the work to recapture the minds of our young men remains plentiful but obtainable.

The importance of a Positive Male Role Model is evident, and according to statistics, the dedication of our men to step forward and make a change has declined. The work to change and restore the lives of our young men in our communities today has become overwhelming and we need your support.

History of the Ultimate Role Model

The Holy Bible

The book of Genesis, chapter 2, verse 15 says, *"Then the Lord God took the man and put him in the garden of Eden to tend and keep it."* When we talk about the history of the male role model, we must start at its origin, the Garden of Eden. This encouraging Bible verse speaks to God's original intent for men. When God created man, He created him with the intention of leading, protecting, and training up young men to follow in his footsteps as he follows God. The man was to be a role model, an example for future generations, mentoring them and teaching them how to maintain and tend to their community.

God did not place Adam in the Garden of Eden simply to relax and have one party after another. Neither was he placed in the Garden of Eden to think only of himself. There was a responsibility placed on him by God Himself; there was continuous work to be done. This responsibility was not to be a strain or burden on Adam but he was to find fulfillment, purpose, and pleasure in following through with what God had ordained him to do.

Deuteronomy, chapter 6, verses 6 through 9 highlight the significance placed on man to embrace God's commandments for his life. He was to let them deeply influence his thoughts and actions. This scripture states that as male role models or leaders of families and communities, they were to impress these thoughts and actions on their children as well. They were to talk about them when they were sitting at home and when they were walking along the roads. They were to have conversations before they laid down and after they got up out of their beds. In other words, men were encouraged to pass down what God had called them to do to future generations through consistent teaching and modeling of God's way in their everyday lives. Of course, we do know that young ladies were being trained and taught as well, but men were to train up young men to be godly men who followed God's way of protecting family and community.

Verse 8 says, *"Tie them as symbols on your hands and bind them on your foreheads."* In other words, it suggests that God's commands should be forever with us, guiding our actions (hands) and our thoughts (forehead), writing them on the doorframes of our homes and on our gates. God is calling man to surround himself and his household with the teachings that He has given him. These verses stress the nature of living out what God had put in place—from personal devotion as men to the passing of that same devotion to young men in hopes that they would one day pass it on to the young men that will come after them. The intention has always been for men to train up the family and community to demonstrate a continuous relationship with God in all aspects of life.

What I Remember

When I think about the command God gave man, the command to be Positive Role Models from the very beginning of mankind, I cannot help but be reminded of the men who were passionate about living this out throughout my community as a young man. The men who often stopped by our home or the once's we saw around our neighborhood, men that I and so many others looked up to as a source of encouragement.

The continuous vision that we saw of hard-working, motivated, and God-fearing men who were living their lives in such a manner that it made us, as young boys and young men, want to imitate and follow. When I think back on those days, it is funny how it was so easy for us young guys to look up to those men in such a way that they literally became our neighborhood heroes. Growing up, I saw men whose sole purpose was to show youngsters how to live life with integrity, hope, compassion, and determination.

These men, or Positive Male Role Models, were significantly affecting the lives of the young men they came in contact with. They played an essential role in the positive development of anyone looking up to them. We were taught how to conduct ourselves in the presence of elders. We were being trained to understand the impact and benefits of work, self-identity, and the importance of being godly men who would one day have the responsibility of protecting, leading, and tending to our own families and communities.

These Positive Male Role Models came into our lives in many ways and in many different forms. They were high school educators who we would see throughout the week. These men would take the time to pour the value of education and social skills into us. They were family members who would take the time to instill family love, self-pride, and self-identity in us. They were neighbors and the fathers of our friends who saw the need to step in and take the place of an absent father. They were pastors and men of the church who took time out to share their testimonies to encourage us to follow Christ. It was even our community leaders who taught us the importance of serving and giving back.

These men did not obtain any favoritism or platform because they were people with fancy lifestyles or personal wealth. These were men of all walks of life who had chosen to be positive role models because they had a burning desire to share with us what God had given them the ability to share, be it advice or skills.

As I look at our young folk today, I can see a major change has taken place. I also see a major change in our men and their desire and willingness to make a difference. Ezekiel 22:30 says that God was searching for a man who would build up the wall and stand in the gap for Him, but He found no one. When I look throughout our communities today for men who are ready to stand in the gap and train up our young men to become Godly men, I do not see many who are willing to lay the foundation like our men in the past did.

Male Role Model Accountability

As men, we are results-oriented creatures. We look for and expect instant results at the time of our actions. Doing something without immediate results can sometimes be a hard pill to swallow, especially if we have to put forth serious effort, go through any form of pain, or be placed in an uncomfortable position.

As a man myself, I wish it worked that way, but unfortunately, that is not how life works for us. As men, we must be prepared to face many obstacles in life that, at the time of action, may not show many signs of the fruit we are expecting to see.

In the home, many times there may be only a few instances where the man hears *"thank you"* or *"we appreciate you."* On the job, it may be the same way; there may be very little fruit outside of pay. Even at the church, many times there seems to be very little reward for the sacrifices you make. For this reason, many are choosing to give up. Many are removing their efforts from the home, from the job, from the community, and even the church. But be reminded today that there is no reward for giving up. Many of our rewards can only be achieved through patience, serious effort, through our pain and suffering, and our being placed in uncomfortable positions.

Many of us are hurting, many are confused, and many are tired. We have suffered; we have faced heartbreak and pain on many levels while searching for the fruit of our labor. And yes, there will still be times when drama enters the home and yes there will also be times when drama shows up on the job, but we cannot continue this cycle of running away and expecting things to fall or stay in place. Our boys need us to start moving different and being better examples, our family and friends need us, and believe it or not, you need you.

Today, I am pleading with those of you who are tired, and I am asking you not to give in. Our young men are suffering and being left to the wolves of life while we, as man, the ones who are supposed to be showing them the way, have dropped the ball and too many are refusing to pick it back up. PICK IT UP.

Everyone hates being uncomfortable; no one wants to be in that position. But it is not meant to make us weak; it is meant to make us stronger. When Christians go through hard times in life, the word of God teaches us that we can find peace in knowing that when we are weak and in doubt, He becomes the strength in which we can rest behind.

Think of the pain while weightlifting. It might hurt, but you are becoming stronger in the process. More weights equal more pain. More pain equals more strength. God is healing and building during the process. Things may get hard sometimes, but you keep searching for peace, joy, and clarity. How do we do that? We seek the wisdom of Christ, our Head Role Model.

I wonder sometimes why so many of our men today have given up on our young kings-to-be. I wonder if, over the years, they have grown tired of talking to a generation of young men who seem to have made up their minds to do whatever they see fit in their own eyes. If that be the case, then I am concerned that we will see a generation of young men incarcerated, dead, or lacking everything that is required to lead anyone, including themselves.

I am also concerned that many of our men today are lacking the ability to be role models because of their unwillingness to grow up and take on the responsibility that God has placed before us as men. 1 Corinthians 13:11 says, *"When I was a child, my speech, feelings, and thinking were all those of a child; now that I am an adult, I have no more use for childish ways."*

I once heard Kobe Bryant say he developed as a ball player in stages. He said, *"When I was a kid, I played basketball for fun. When I was a teenager, I played to win. But when I became a man, I played to be my best. Whether I won or lost, my goal was to always give my best effort."* The hard question that we, as men, must ask ourselves today is, *"What stage are we in? Are you living to have fun, are you living to win, or are you living to do your best and be your best?"*

We have too many men living their lives today only concerned about having fun, and it has taken its toll on our boys. They are not taking life seriously; everything about life must be fun and games and come easy. They do not want the responsibility of leading a young man in the proper way because it takes focus and effort. They do not want the pressure that comes with being a role model in today's world, and this is bleeding into our young men, causing our homes, families, and communities to suffer.

Many of our young men today have begun to follow in the footsteps of these weak men, embracing these bad habits and feeling that life should be fun and games. When things don't go their way, they cannot cope with reality and decide that shutting down or violence is the answer.

Then there are those men that are living to win. These bad influences, not role models, will do anything and everything they must in order to win. They are not concerned about others, how they feel, or what they are going through; their only concern is getting what they want when they want it.

Many of our young men today have taken on this bad habit as well and feel like they must win by any means necessary. They feel they must have their way in every aspect of life. They are lacking the wisdom of knowing that as men, there will be MANY times in life when we will have to make sacrifices for others. It is best that boys be taught that sometimes we will have to take the short end of the stick for others to benefit. Any real man will agree.

The work is plentiful, and I thank God for the men who are trying to do their very best to continue what our forefathers started. These Positive Male Role Models are doing what they can throughout our communities to reach and teach our young men. They understand how important it is for our young men to have morals, self-motivation, self-love, self-respect, and respect for others. They understand how important it is to the family and community that we rush to make a difference because we have blind men blazing trails and paving roads of destruction that are leading our boys away from God and into total disaster.

We, as men, must come out of that fun stage. We must move from that stage of needing to win and seek to be our very best. The only way we can truly be our best is to follow God's plan for us. I feel that if we are going to save our boys, it must start in the same way that God instructed Jesus to start in His search. God was and is looking for men with humble hearts—men who will sacrifice everything for the same cause that Christ had and who will stand in the gap as servant-leaders for their families and for His plan.

Mr. R. Coleman put it this way in his book, *"Master Plan of Evangelism"*: *"It all started by Jesus calling a few men to follow Him...His concern was not with programs to reach the multitudes, but with men whom the multitudes would follow...Men were to be His method of winning the world to God."*

As men, we need an intentional strategy to reach men because if you reach a man, you reach his whole family. A changed man will influence a marriage and a family. A changed family will influence a neighborhood and a community. A changed community will influence a state and a nation. A changed nation will help change the world. It all begins with a changed man.

I think we can all agree that the foundation is the most important part of building any structure. You don't start with the roof, rafters, or window frames. To obtain any strong structure that will stand against any major weather, it's going to require that your foundation be right. God works the same way with humanity. He is the true MASTER BUILDER. If you look at 1 Timothy 2:13, you will find that God made Adam first (that's the foundation) and afterward He made Eve.

Why do you think God did this? It was because God is a God of order, and He was signifying that the man is the foundation on which the family should be built, on which the community should be built, and on which the church should be built.

It is time to check the foundation because when we look around at our world today, it seems the floods have come in and the winds are blowing, and our homes are falling apart. The structure, the beauty, and the safety of our communities are caving in. Our church principles are deteriorating, and our young men seem to be losing their minds because they are looking for something solid to stand on, and many times all they find is sand.

Most of us are football fans, as for me, I watch my sure of football during the season, and what I have come to realize is that regardless of how well the receivers run their routes, regardless of how well the running backs hold on to the ball, regardless of how well the coaches call the plays, everything comes down to the quarterbacks and how well they have prepared themselves.

Everything comes down to how well they know the playbook, how well they are able to motivate the guys around them because they know they are the team's foundation, and they have to be willing to lay it all on the line if they are going to have any chance at winning the game.

Many men today have left the home and the upbringing of the boys to the women, and many of our woman have taking on that challenge and with Gods help, they are making it work. But we as real men of God must never settle for this. It does not matter how well the wife is running with the ball, it does not matter how well the kids are running their routes, it does not matter how well God is calling the plays for us as men. If we, as men, haven't gotten deep into that godly playbook and learned the plays, if we are not willing to be obedient, if we are not willing to be self-motivated, and make the sacrifices for the team—whoever that team may be (sons, nephews, brothers, cousins, grandsons)—how can we win the game?

Real Life Short Stories

The winter snow in Washington, D.C., always reminds me of the boys who lived next door. There were three of them. They would shovel my sidewalk, the youngest trying his hardest to keep up with his two older brothers. When I first moved to the neighborhood, their father urged them to help me with the heavy boxes or carry my groceries inside. He kept a close watch over them, warning his boys of the dangers that lurked in the streets.

Then their father died, and life became dramatically different for these boys next door. Our neighborhood, less than four miles from the U.S. Capitol, is one of the most neglected areas of the city. Here, 73 percent of children live in households headed by a woman. There is high poverty and unemployment, devastating crime and violence, substance abuse and homelessness, and rising rates of high school dropouts and teenage pregnancy.

Far too often, gunshots pierce the dark quiet nights, followed by police sirens and ambulance horns. At times, helicopters hover above, trying to find the thieves that steal lives.

It is in this place, littered with check-cashing storefronts, liquor stores, and carryout joints, where mothers struggle to both make ends meet and keep their children safe. And it is in this place where too many black boys, like the boys next door, must navigate life alone.

Not long after their father's death, the boys started skipping school and missing curfew. Typical teenage behavior turned into serious crime. More than once, I witnessed one of the boys being led away in handcuffs by police. Their mother, for her part, sought help from the school system, the courts, and the government.

But her efforts fell short. None of the boys graduated from high school. Two have been in the criminal justice system, and the youngest has had several stints in drug rehab. So, what happened? Would their lives have been different if their father had lived? What did these young men need in their lives that their mother could not provide?

***

Boone grew up in a neighborhood where in-home fathers did not exist, he says. The few who were physically present were not there spiritually or emotionally. *"I never saw dads in the park playing with their sons,"* Boone recalls.

In his own life, Boone, a native of Brooklyn, N.Y., says that his father was present but not there. A star high school basketball player, Boone says his father came to only one of his games. *"I don't remember my father hugging me. We never heard him say he was proud of us,"* Boone says of himself and his brother. *"The emotional pain of what I deserve and did not get, I have to carry it for the rest of my life."*

***

Beaty carried the pain of his father's absence due to incarceration. He described the lingering emotions in his poem, "Knock, Knock":

... 25 years later I write these words for the little boy in me who still awaits his dad's knock ... Dad, come home, because there are things that I do not know and I thought maybe you could teach me: how to shave, how to dribble a ball, how to talk to a girl, how to walk like a man...

25 years later a little boy cries and so I write these words and try to heal and try to father myself and I dream up a father who says the words that my father did not ...

***

Barack Obama has talked about the "hole" in his heart left by the absence of his father. In February 2014, Obama announced My Brother's Keeper. The initiative works to expand opportunities for boys and young men of color in underserved communities with a focus on education, reading, job training, and mentoring.

"*I believe the continuing struggles of so many boys and young men—the fact that too many of them are falling by the wayside, dropping out, unemployed, involved in negative behavior, going to jail, being profiled—this is a moral issue for our country,*" said Obama at the time of the announcement.

***

In Clemmons, N.C., right outside Winston-Salem, Ms. Porter is looking for a mentor for her 14-year-old son, Jalen. "*He has never had his dad in his life,*" says Porter, 43. "*His father does not call. He does not see him.*" Porter and her son's father divorced after three years of marriage.

Her former husband moved to Connecticut, and she moved to North Carolina to be closer to family. Around the time Jalen was 7 or 8, Porter says, she started seeing changes in her son. He became violent and acted out in school. "*He stayed in the principal's office,*" Porter says. In one year, Jalen was moved to three different schools. "*He was just angry at everything and everyone.*"

"*He actually tried to hurt himself,*" Porter remembers. "*He was always crying. You had to wrap your arms around him and rock him.*" Porter sought help from mental health professionals, and Jalen was diagnosed with depression, mood disorder, and attention deficit/hyperactivity disorder. He sees a therapist and psychiatrist. They have said that father absence may be a contributing factor, says Porter. *"I do understand he wants a father so bad. He wants a complete family,"* Porter says.

The holidays are especially difficult. And Jalen has gotten used to his father not calling on his birthday. But seeing his friends with their fathers only makes him more upset, says Porter. *"His father can go a whole year without contacting me or checking on his kids,"* Porter notes. *"He feels a sense of abandonment by his dad."*

With her former husband not stepping up, however, Porter tried to enlist her 70-year-old father to help with her son. But as a senior citizen, Jalen's grandfather could only do so much with his teen grandson. So, Porter signed up for Big Brothers Big Sisters. *"He got paired with a young man—24 years old,"* says Porter. *"He has not called Jalen yet."* She pulled her son from the program because she did not want him disappointed again. But as Jalen gets older, Porter says, she needs help. *"I need some male mentors for my son, someone to show him how to be a man,"* she says. *"I am trying to keep him out of the judicial system, keep him from being the angry black male that goes out in society."*

On the rare occasions when Jalen and his father meet, Porter notes, Jalen is a different person. *"He melts like butter,"* says Porter. *"It is a look of 'I want to be around you, but I don't know if I can trust you.'"*

Interviewer #1

Question 1: What is a Positive Male Role Model?

Interviewer number 1 stated that he believes a positive male role model is a person who carries himself in a way that inspires others to emulate them. Their character aligns with someone else's need for guidance, creating a dynamic where one leads and the other follows.

Question 2: Did you have a Positive Male Role Model in your life? What were the effects of it on you?

Interviewer number 1 shared that he did have a Positive Male Role Model in his life. He explained that his parents divorced when he was 2 years old. Although he visited his father occasionally, he was never able to build a strong bond with him.

"My big brother was who I looked up to for years," he said. "He was 13 years older than I was, and I remember him carrying me around on his shoulders as a child. He was my protection and my hero, all rolled into one."

Interviewer number 1 mentioned that his brother left for the Army when he was around 6 years old, and he vividly remembers feeling sick to his stomach when his brother left.

He continued, "My brother would call and check on me every week, but I still felt alone. Everything changed for me when I attended church with my mom one Sunday and was introduced to a man named Brother Michael." Brother Michael was a Deacon in the church, known for spending time with the boys in the community.

As we sat there talking, I could see his eyes begin to water up just thinking about those days. He said, "I have friends who are still dealing with drug issues, criminal issues, and job issues to this day, but I credit my big brother and Brother Michael for stepping in and teaching me what it means to be a responsible man." He concluded by saying, "If there were more Brother Michaels around nowadays, these youngsters wouldn't be as wild and uncaring as they are."

Question 3: Are you a Positive Male Role Model? Why or why not?

When I asked Interviewer number 1 if he considered himself a positive male role model, he said that he has tried over the years to be a positive influence on the boys and young men in his neighborhood, but nowadays, they don't seem to want anyone telling them anything. He makes sure to spend valuable time with his sons and nephews to ensure they don't get caught up in the streets.

Interviewer number 1 emphasized that he understands how important it is for men to fight for black boys, even if they don't want to fight for themselves. He knows they are lost and cannot see or understand the breakdown happening in our communities. He hopes that more fathers will take responsibility for their roles as fathers.

Interviewer #2

Question 1: What is a Positive Male Role Model?

When Interviewer number 2 was asked what he thought a positive male role model was, he said it was someone who takes the time to help others stay on the right track. A role model shows others what to do and what not to do.

Question 2: Did you have a Positive Male Role Model in your life? What were the effects of it?

When Interviewer number 2 was asked if he had a positive male role model growing up, he replied that he had an uncle who tried to talk to him. However, since he believed that was his father's job, he didn't listen much to what his uncle was trying to say. He mentioned that his uncle was a gang member who was in and out of trouble but always encouraged him to do the right thing.

Interviewer number 2 said he saw the respect his uncle had in the streets and thought that was what being a man was all about. Instead of heeding his uncle's plea to do the right thing, he patterned himself after him. After spending a few stints in juvenile centers, his mom reached out to a family friend named Mr. Mike.

"Mr. Mike owned a detail shop in our neighborhood," Interviewer number 2 told me. "*He gave me a job for the summer, and that was the best summer I think I've ever had in my life.*" Mr. Mike taught him all about detailing cars and working hard. "*I watched how he talked with people and how everyone respected him, both hardworking people and people in the streets. I owe everything I am and everything I have to Mr. Mike.*"

Interviewer number 2 shared that after spending four years working for Mr. Mike, Mr. Mike fell ill. "*One morning, I came into work, and he sat me down and told me he wouldn't be able to continue working. He handed me the keys to the shop and told me he wanted me to have it on one condition: that I promise to do for someone else what he had done for me.*"

Question 3: Are you a Positive Male Role Model? Why or why not?

When I asked Interviewer number 2 if he was a positive male role model, he said he sure hoped so. He mentioned that he made a promise to Mr. Mike that he would do for someone else everything that Mr. Mike had done for him. "*Mr. Mike passed away about two years later, around 12 years ago,*" he recalled.

Interviewer number 2 explained that he has taken in a young man to work for him every summer since he took over the shop. He prides himself on the fact that five of the young men he has mentored have gone on to college, and three have joined the military. He wishes more business owners would take young black boys under their wings and show them something different, the same way Mr. Mike did for him and the way he is doing for others. *"I am living proof that it works,"* he said.

Interviewer #3

Question 1: What is a Positive Male Role Model?

Interviewer number 3 was a special interview because she spoke from a woman/mother's point of view. When asked what she thought a positive male role model was, she replied, "A role model is someone, male or female, who brings someone into their life. A role model helps to develop a person's mind and shape their character. They show they care; not just say they care."

Question 2: Have you or your child ever had an experience with a Positive Male Role Model? If so, what was that experience like?

Interviewer number 3 stated that her son's father was her son's positive male role model and that he was always there for her son, Wayne. She said that everywhere he went, he always had Wayne with him. However, when Wayne was 10 years old, his father was killed in an accident. She recalled how devastated she had to tell her son that his best friend, his everything, was gone.

"Hurt cannot begin to explain it," she said. *"He/they were down for the count."*

She explained that everything began to go downhill quickly—his grades, his attitude, and his social life all plummeted. He didn't want to go anywhere or be around anyone. She reached out to his father's brother, thinking it might help the situation, but his patience was short, and he was gone as fast as he came.

It was when she saw Brother Steve working with some of the other boys that she decided to reach out to him and explain their issue. Interviewer number 3 said, "Brother Steve sat down and listened to my son. He called him, checked on him at school. It was like Brother Steve needed Wayne as much as Wayne needed Brother Steve."

"It took some time to break down the wall my son had built up, but Brother Steve came, and he stayed. It has been six years now, and Wayne's grades are great. He's a star athlete, he works in the community, he's an Eagle Scout, and he will tell anybody who will sit and listen long enough that there ain't nobody like his Uncle Steve, as he calls him."

So, to answer the question about our experience with role models, she concluded, *"I can only say my son's role model was Heaven-sent."*

Interviewer #4

Question 1: What is a Positive Male Role Model?

This question was posed to a 15-year-old Black teenager. He thinks that a positive male role model is somebody you can depend on. He says that role models teach you how to be stable and make good decisions. They show you the difference between right and wrong and they hold you accountable.

Question 2: Do you have a Positive Male Role Model?

This young man said that he has two positive male role models. He said his positive role models are his father and his basketball coach. His dad is a truck driver and is often on the road for two or three weeks at a time, but his coach promised his dad that he would look out for him while he was away.

This young man stated that without his dad and coach being in his life, he didn't know where he would be. "I have tried to hang out with the knuckleheads," he said, "but my dad talked to my coach, and they both said that I can't do both. Either I get my lesson and listen to my mom, or basketball is out of the question." He added that he knows they want the best for him and his little brother, and if he listens to what they are trying to teach him, he will grow to be a great man.

Question 3: Do you think that Positive Male Role Models are important? If so, how?

The teenager said that he wished all the guys in his school had positive role models. He stated that many of the boys are doing things they would not do if they had somebody taking time up with them. He spoke about a young man he knows who is only 15 years old, yet already has a baby, sells drugs, and hangs out in the streets.

He said they used to play Pee Wee baseball together when they were younger, but when they were about 12 years old, his mom stopped him from hanging out with the young man because he was getting into too much trouble at school. He mentioned that the boy's dad was in jail and expressed that he wished the boy had a role model. However, he then added that the boy probably wouldn't listen to anything a role model had to say now, because he's too caught up in the world.

A Hand to Guide Me

Many of the people we see and admire today have been influenced by someone. In the book *A Hand to Guide Me*, Denzel Washington showcases how the kindness and influence of mentors and role models have shaped the lives of people who are now considered legends. In their own words, these well-known personalities tell how others stepped up to guide them. *"Everyone needs a hand from time to time,"* Denzel says. *"A gentle nudge to get on track—you never know when the help you provide will lift someone towards a life of greatness."*

Denzel Washington begins by quoting, *"Train up a child in the way he should go, and when he is old, he will not depart from it."*

He says he is amazed at how many people soon lose sight of this. *"Show me a successful individual, and I'll show you someone who didn't want for positive influence in his or her life,"* says Mr. Washington.

"We are all destined to leave some kind of mark. I really believe that. We are all meant to walk a certain path at a certain time, in a certain direction, for a certain purpose. But we sometimes miss our marks, and without a certain push from a positive role model or mentor in the right direction, we might never find the path we were meant to follow."

Hank Aaron, a retired professional baseball player, says that his mother, father, aunts, and uncles raised him. He didn't have to look far for a role model because in the small town of Mobile, Alabama, where he was raised, everybody knew everybody, and everybody knew everybody's kids. He says his uncle Bubba developed him into the man and ballplayer he became by spending time with him on a day-to-day basis.

Muhammad Ali, a retired boxer and activist, says that although he had a father in his life as a boy, he didn't meet his role model until after he had become an adult and retired from boxing in 1981. He says that after meeting Nelson Mandela in person, learning his story, and spending countless hours with him, Mandela became not only his role model but also his hero.

Michael Vick, a retired professional football player, says that it was because of a man named Poo Johnson, the executive director of the Boys and Girls Club in Newport News, Virginia, where he grew up. Vick says he was at the club all the time, and Mr. Poo was always there too. Vick noted that he never understood why, but Mr. Poo took a liking to him and never let him sell himself short. Vick says he would try to dodge Mr. Poo from time to time, but everywhere he looked, there he was. "It's like there were six or seven of him, and each one was watching out for me," Vick says.

Better Dads, Stronger Sons

Our boys will have a greater chance of becoming strong, dedicated, and prepared men if strong, dedicated, and prepared men show them the way.

Mentor and Masculinity

Better, Dads, Stronger Sons is an insightful book written by Rick Johnson. It contains the knowledge and wisdom of men and women who have not only studied the breakdown in relationships between fathers and boys in our communities but also share life experiences related to this subject. Mr. Johnson begins by stating that boys become men by watching men, by standing close to men. He explains that manhood is a ritual passed from generation to generation with precious few spoken instructions.

I can personally relate to Mr. Johnson's point. I remember the men in past generations being quiet but effective in getting their point across. Mr. Johnson goes on to say that passing the torch of manhood is a fragile and tedious task. If the rite of passage is successfully completed, the boy becomes a Godly man, and during his life, his influence will bless all those fortunate enough to lean on him and rest under his canopy.

Boys can only become men through the influence of other men, emphasizing that masculinity bestows masculinity, and that femininity can never bestow masculinity. I believe many women have done and continue to do great jobs raising their boys, but there is a point where a man's influence becomes necessary, whether it be positive or negative.

John Eldredge says, "A boy learns who he is and what he's about from a man or the company of men. He cannot learn it from any other place. He cannot learn it from other mislead boys, and he cannot learn it from the words or actions of women." I completely agree with Eldredge's point. So many young men in our communities are lost, not knowing who they are or who they were created to be.

Eldredge shares a few things he believes are necessary to correct this issue.

He begins by stating that it requires active intervention in a boy's life by a positive adult male. Without that intervention in the form of a positive male role model, boys are like ships without rudders, tossed about whichever way the wind and waves of culture throw them.

In her book, *Between Mothers and Sons: The Making of Vital and Loving Men*, Evelyn Bassoff writes, "When a boy has no flesh-and-blood men with whom to identify, he may turn his inspiration to the pitiful images the popular media promotes, like the neighborhood gang leaders or criminals whose brutality they mistake for true masculinity." I think we can all agree that many of our homes and communities are full of young men who have found their footing under the leadership of gang and criminal influence.

There is a question that boys will ask themselves at some point in their lives. It is a question many of us found ourselves wondering as boys. A boy has a void in his soul that asks, "Am I a man? How will I know? Am I tough enough? Do I run fast enough or jump high enough? Am I strong enough?" Eldredge says, "It's not a question—it's *the* only question, the one every boy and some men long to know the answer to: Do I have what it takes? Am I powerful?" These questions must be answered at some point.

Until a man knows he is a man, he will forever be trying to prove it while simultaneously shrinking from anything that might resemble one. Most men live their lives haunted by that question or have become crippled by the answer they have been given.

Boys need that void filled by the actions and blessings of another man. A woman can tell her son all day long that he is normal, that he is strong, that he is capable, but he will never truly believe her. However, when another male gives him the answers to those questions that have been planted deep in his heart, they will be readily, and with relief, believed.

Dads and Positive Male Role Models are the biggest factors in making that transformation possible. In his book *Man Enough*, Frank Pittman states, "It must be male to male. No matter how wonderful or loving a woman is, she can't teach a boy everything he needs to know."

We both agree, as do many of you, I'm sure, that young men should have fathers, grandfathers, uncles, or stepfathers to raise them from boys into men. If you do not have men in our families, then you must find positive men for your boys to follow after so we can continue bridging this gap that lay between OUR boys and US as black men!

If the only males our young men know are other teenage boys in the community or the fake heroes from the movies, they will more times than not develop a distorted, exaggerated concept of masculinity.

The fact that boys and some men, if I am going to be real about it, need positive male role models. They not only need men to model appropriate behaviors but also men who are willing to actively mentor them.

As a father, our primary responsibility to our sons is to model the behaviors of positive masculinity and then provide that boy with the knowledge it takes to become a godly man and father through your mentoring or raising process. Steve Farrar says, "It is my God-appointed task to ensure that my sons will be ready to lead a family. I must equip them to that end."

Little boys are the hope of the next generation. They are the fathers of tomorrow. They must be taught who they are and what their responsibilities, as men will be. They must see their role models in action. Boys who grow up without healthy men in their lives face serious disadvantages later in life. They should not have to take on the task of discovering on their own what it takes to become a man—a huge and frightening task.

This book, along with other data, points out those boys who grow up fatherless and without a positive male role model more often than not end up jobless, godless, and dangerous. Not only do they fail to understand their roles as providers and protectors of their families, but also they are also afraid to pursue a life of significance.

Boys who don't receive male guidance many times are confused about their roles in life, rarely finding true security or satisfaction. So many of our young men today are living insecure and unsatisfied lives because they did not receive or adhere to what a man was trying to instill in them. An important advantage a boy gains from having and listening to a positive male role model is the ability to pursue the life he was meant to live.

Every son wants to gain a sense of mission in life and receive the blessing from an respected male figure (preferably his father) to pursue that mission—to feel strong, loving, and masculine with the ground beneath his feet so that he will not, once he's an adult, have to say to his wife, to his children, or to anyone for that matter, "I do not know what a man is. Please teach me." And such is the dilemma that many men face today—they have grown up never really knowing what it means to be a Godly man or father.

A son is truly blessed when his father is present in his life. Boys also need other men besides their fathers in their lives helping to steer them in the right direction.

In earlier times, most men accepted the responsibility for teaching boys to become men. In fact, in biblical times, it was a father's responsibility to find other male mentors for his son, as he grew older. Other men that would expose the boy to different jobs and skills in hopes that he would find interest in one. *When the father was gone, other men stepped in. When the father was not known, other men stepped up to protect and provide for them, ensuring that the females and children were taken care of. When the young boys came of age, these men mentored them through the social and emotional challenges of life."*

Imagine if we, as men, had kept that important way of life going where men stepped in and supported the women by assuring them that their boys would grow to become productive and Godly men.

The custom from the Old Testament that if a man is killed or dies his brother should marry his wife, would not fly in our day, nonetheless it was a nurturing strategy required by a society that knew the risks of a lost father.

The Power of Fathers and Male Role Models

Better, Dads, Stronger Sons makes a great point when it elaborates on how fathers receive their power from God and set out to transfer this to their sons. Are fathers and positive male role models really all that important?

Dr. James Dobson, one of the contributors asked to give his studied opinion for this dynamic book, believes that our very survival as a people depends on the presence or absence of masculine leadership in millions of homes across the country. He stated something very powerful when he said, "Being a good father is not so much about what kind of parent you are as it is about what kind of person you are. What kind of character do you have? How do you approach life and your responsibilities as a father? What are you allowing your son to see in you and what are you allowing him to be exposed to in the world?"

Fathers have an innate ability to influence their children, especially their boys, and the community around them. Dr. Dobson calls it "Father/Manpower." This is not the physical power of being bigger and stronger than their wives and kids, but the generational power with which God has endowed them—the power that allows fathers, and men in general, to affect people's lives positively or negatively, for good or bad. Whether a man knows it or not, he will impact the lives of those around him. It doesn't matter if he is intentional with it or not; men are created to make an impact.

If we, as men, do not hurry up and commit to training up our boys, we will continue dealing with the angry, out-of-control young men that we face today, as well as putting our daughters in the position of raising fatherless children.

I agree with Dr. Dobson when he says he does not want to have to explain to God someday that he ignored all these boys who needed his attention only because he was more interested in his own needs and desires.

Young men under 25 in this country are approaching masculine meltdown. Because of a lack of positive male role models in their lives, they have no idea what a man is, how a man acts, how he feels, or what he lives for."

Rick Johnson, says that in their rage against their fatherless "wounds," young men often commit acts of violence. Boys without a positive male role model in their lives often have no accountability. They tend to react according to their own notions about life, living in a world of fantasy, as if to say, "It's them against the world."

Older men have a responsibility to walk alongside younger men, giving them the benefit of their experience. Likewise, young men should be open—in fact, eager—to receive advice from the more mature members of their gender. Too often, however, male pride on both sides stops them from sharing and receiving this crucial information.

It is important that men begin reaching out to other boys and young men to mentor; our responsibility as men and fathers does not stop with our sons. The fact is that if we do not curb the multitude of young men entering adulthood without proper training in how to be real godly men, fathers, and husbands, our culture will continue to plunder.

As hard as it may be for some to believe, many young men today are desperately seeking positive role models to tell them the secrets to living life as a healthy, production, and Godly man in today's environment. If we only knew how important we are in the lives of young men and boys, we would not be so reluctant to step in and give them the benefit of our experience.

Why do you think women make up 85 percent of single parents in our country? Approximately 50 percent of the children in this country will live at least a portion of their growing-up years in a single-parent home. Today, 30 percent of children are born out of wedlock. Nearly 90 percent of all violent crime is committed by men raised by single mothers. At least 70 percent of men in prison are from fatherless homes or lacked a one-on-one connection with a positive male to confide in.

This book makes it very clear that these statistics are not a put down or belittling of women. It is a bullseye that reflects the position of our black men right now. We are the ones who have dropped the ball and failed in our God-given responsibilities. It is up to us, as a collective people, to stop this trend and get real about raising up a generation of black boys and young men who will revive us.

Some of our young men may indeed be lost, but as we have seen, with the right programs and men with the right attitudes and desires, we can restore our boys. But we must be willing to put in the time needed for these boys. We must remain active in their lives.

I understand that there are times when a father may not be as involved in his son's life as he would like to be, especially right after a tough divorce or a nasty breakup. However, that does not change the importance or the fact that without a father's influence and guidance, children—especially sons—will have to face overwhelming obstacles without the support of their hero.

The struggles with life that they carry with them will likely wreak havoc on those around them—especially when they become adults, have kids, and began passing that pain and disorder down to the generations that follow. The sad thing about it is they may all have to suffer from something you helped create. I think they are worth fighting for, even enduring some difficult circumstances for, don't you?

As men, we sometimes use the term, "take one for the team." Well, in this case, men, we must be willing to take whatever comes our way to be a part of our children's lives, especially our sons'. Take one for the family.

Research

When we watch the news or move about in our communities, we are constantly reminded of how damaged many young men have become. There are so many challenges they face when a positive male role model is not present, affecting various aspects of their lives.

The presence of a positive male role model shapes their values and ethics. Positive male role models play an indispensable role in helping boys develop their moral compass. They demonstrate the importance of integrity, honesty, and empathy, instilling values that create a just and compassionate society. Without these influences, boys may struggle to relate to the significance of these virtues, potentially leading to low morals and maturity confusion.

Personal growth and self-esteem in young men are often cultivated through identification and association. The lack of male role models can leave boys grappling with self-doubt and insecurity. Many of the young men we see in our communities are lost as to who they really are and what they can achieve. Without an active positive male role model in their lives, most will question their worth and capabilities, pointing back to the absence of that guiding hand that should have been there to reassure them of their potential.

Career aspirations and ambitions are often shaped and developed by the influence of role models whether they be good or bad. Taking the time to get involved and building communication with our boys helps them visualize their future through your character and opinion. Positive male role models provide insight into different career paths, instill a sense of ambition, and offer guidance on how to achieve their dreams. In their absence, boys may struggle to set meaningful goals, limiting their professional potential.

In the presence of positive male role models, young men learn about emotional intelligence through real-life examples. Boys who lack such influences may find it challenging to navigate their emotions effectively, potentially leading to issues such as anger management problems, depression, mental health struggles, or criminal and drug addiction. These issues are starting to manifest at younger ages than ever before.

The Impact of Absent Fathers on the Mental Health of Black Boys

Lottie L. Joiner, a Washington, D.C.-based freelance writer, wrote about the impact of absent male role models on the mental health of Black boys while participating in the National Health Journalism Fellowship, a program of the University of Southern California's Annenberg School of Journalism.

What I found through these studies is the fact that youths in father-absent households have the highest odds of being incarcerated, higher levels of behavioral problems in schools, and are more likely to be suspended from school. Research by Princeton University sociology professor Sara McLanahan notes that a father's absence increases anti-social behavior such as drug use and reduces a child's chances of employment.

Many of the issues our young men face today stem from their fathers leaving them at an early age. This does not excuse or justify breaking laws or participating in drug use. I am only stating that male guidance and presence are major factors in the life of a boy.

Absent fathers and the lack of positive male role models are the strongest indicators of delinquency, even more so than low socioeconomic status or peer pressure. There is also evidence that fatherless children have lower self-esteem, a greater risk for mental illness and suicide, and an increased risk of depression.

Organizations such as 100 Black Men of America, Disciples Brotherhood of Tylertown, MS, Youth Villages of Hattiesburg, MS, The Power of One Outreach Ministry of Brookhaven, MS, and Big Brothers Big Sisters of America are working very hard in our areas to address some of the issues fatherless boys may encounter through mentoring and male enrichment programs. The question that I would like to pose to you is this, what is taking place in your community to combat these damaging issues?

The Mental Stress of Being Fatherless

Who's taking care of the hearts and minds of boys hurt by the absence of a father figure?

Although numerous organizations address the social implications of growing up without a father, how can the community address the psychological impact of fatherlessness? Leon Caldwell, senior research director at Think Shift, a Washington, D.C.-based social innovation collaborative of the DeBruce Foundation, acknowledges that there may be a lack of mental-health practitioners in this space. However, he points out that after-school programs—such as those found at the Boys & Girls Club of America or mentoring organizations like Mentoring USA—create the space and time to assess a young person's mental health and well-being.

"During your interaction with a youth, you can ask, 'How are you feeling? How are your grades? Who are your friends in school?' Most times, if asked, they will tell you if they are frustrated or agitated," says Caldwell, who has designed and evaluated programming for organizations that focus on African-American boys.

We must understand that relationships are everything. With the proper relationship established between the two parties, we know and have seen growth develop in our boys. But without relationship building, there is little to no growth, leaving our young men running wild.

In her research, Professor Faye Belgrave found that a father's involvement is more important than his presence in the home. Simply put, seeing he is not enough; seeing he is only the beginning of the process, he must be hands-on. It is not the father's absence from the home that matters as much as his quality involvement with his child.

I can remember dealing with the issue of my father not being in the home with me at the most crucial time of my life—my teens. Even though I knew, he was a phone call away, not being able to see him often because he lived 800 miles away made life challenging. So, family structure does not matter as much to a boy if he has quality time and positive involvement with his father or a positive male role model.

Connecting Fathers with Their Children

A number of organizations—including Mississippi Fathers and Families Coalition of America, Tomorrow's Fathers of Meridian, MS, and Disciples Brotherhood of Tylertown, MS—work to connect fathers with their children. Fathers Incorporated programs are designed to help raise awareness of the importance of positive male role models. These programs also introduce parents to different ways they can improve and develop healthy father-child relationships.

Jawanza Kunjufu, the author of several books on African-American boys, including the 2007 best-seller *Raising Black Boys*, was asked to give his thoughts concerning our boys and the men in or out of their lives. Mr. Kunjufu calls it "posttraumatic missing daddy disorder." He said that most boys are not going to be honest and say, "I'm really hurting because I'm missing my daddy." A mentor once a week is extremely important, but there is no one that a boy wants to please more than his father.

Boone, from *The Real Stories*, remembers his father taking him to pool halls and prostitution houses, but he didn't care. "Even though my dad was bad, I just wanted to be around him," says Boone. "Even with him beating my mother, taking me into pool halls, at the end of the day, he was still my father. I wanted my father, but he never allowed me to be his son."

Porter says she knows that her son longs to see his father more often, but her former husband's absence has taken an emotional toll on her as she tries to find her son the resources to thrive. "I feel like I'm going through this by myself," says Porter. "It has become a struggle for me. It has been tough."

Caldwell says that there was a time when there were men and institutions, such as the church, in the Black community that guided young men—but not so much anymore. Caldwell goes on to say that structurally, we must look at how we support people in the ecosystem where Black boys live.

Black males need a nurturing environment. That is not to say the environment should be soft or that anything should be freely given, but it should be a nurturing environment that helps restore faith and trust in humanity. Our community has stopped creating those nurturing environments. Our communities have become fragmented. Neighborhoods have been decimated due to a lack of economic opportunity.

As a result, Black boys' aimlessness ends up in hopeless positions, and many who really want out are left to deal with the ongoing violence in many urban areas. If a community has nothing to develop the minds of our boys, if it has no one to bridge the gap for absent fathers, then how can we expect our young men to do anything but fail?

Ministries' such as *Disciples Brotherhood in Tylertown, MS*, The Power of One Outreach Ministry in Brookhaven, MS, and Boys to Men Program in Hazlehurst, MS have taken steps in the right direction in terms of addressing some of the issues relating to absent fathers and absent positive male role models. Many Church youth and men ministries certainly make a difference in the lives of our boys. Coaches and trainers also play an important role in getting boys off the street. But sadly, there is still plenty of work to be done.

We are thankful for the positive men willing to be father figures, coaches, and role models, and you guys are doing great jobs. Many of you moms are doing great jobs as well but we cannot afford to let this fire die down. We must keep these conversations on the floor because 72 percent of black children still have absent fathers or father figures, not to mention that 5 million of those black children or black boys. And in many cases, we have found that their village is not strong enough, big enough, or committed enough.

Absent Fathers Aren't a Barrier to Success

Wizdom Powell, an associate professor of health behavior at the University of North Carolina's Gillings School of Global Public Health, warns against the notion that Black men need fathers to be successful. She clarifies that she is not arguing that fathers are unimportant or that they do not play a critical role. However, she believes that society tends to build up the role of Black fathers to a place of completeness and, in turn, minimize the abilities of the Black mothers to build up King's. When we suggest that boys cannot be healthy and whole without their fathers, it inadvertently implies that mothers are somehow insufficient.

The tone a mother sets around a father's absence—whether due to death, incarceration, or a lack of presence in child-rearing—also plays a significant role in a boy's emotional and mental well-being.

"I think it is how we set up that relationship and how we frame his father's absence that makes the most impact. We have to think about how to create a community of positive male role models who can step in and provide the support boys need from a male figure," she explains.

"One of the biggest challenges boys face when it comes to a father's absence, or the absence of a positive male role model, is the lack of someone to teach them how to think from a male perspective—how to manage and catalyze anger productively, and all of the rules around emotional functioning that they need to lean on to succeed. Without a positive male guide, this can create a socioemotional void, even if there is not a physical void."

Mrs. Belgrave and I both agree that parents must establish proper structures for their sons and closely monitor their activities. Sports and rites-of-passage programs have proven to provide opportunities for positive male involvement. It should not be left up to the child to decide whom they spend time with. As a parent, you should approve of the friends your child associates with, know the parents of those friends, and be aware of how and where they spend their time. It only takes being part of a negative peer group for a child to get off track.

Thabiti Boone, like many others, found his male role model on the basketball court. His high school coach saw potential in him and guided him through his struggles.

"He understood the impact and pain I was dealing with from not having my father around," says Boone. "He helped me cope with that."

Boone has served as a White House Champion of Change for his work on fatherhood issues. He has also served as the international representative for Omega Psi Phi Fraternity's fatherhood and mentoring initiative. Additionally, Boone assists the NBA with service projects and acts as an advisor to Fathers and Men of Professional Basketball Players Inc. Yet despite his success, Boone admits that he still yearns for his father's love.

"I wanted to work hard in hopes that I would somehow receive the love, value, and appreciation of my father," Boone writes. He was a teen father himself, who took his daughter to college with him and gave up a promising NBA career. "I've learned to take the love I didn't have from him and turn it into my passion to be a leader in fatherhood. Fathers need to know that their sons need them so that they can be emotionally stable."

Father Abandonment:

DEAR ABSENTEE,

That name means you should be here, but you are not. When you left, pieces of my life went with you. I needed to know that I could count on you. We were supposed to build something together—lots of things together. You could have played with me. That would have helped my confidence grow. You could have been there to build me up after a hard day at school. Instead, I got really mad. You could have helped me build important life skills. Mom is doing her best to fill the piece that was always meant for you. Because there are some things, only a dad can do.

Signed, THE CHILD WHO NEVER KNEW YOU.

Parents have a sacred duty to rear their children in love and righteousness. By divine design, fathers are to preside over their families in love and righteousness and are responsible for providing the necessities of life and protection for their families. There are significant negative effects when these duties are neglected by absent fathers or the lack of positive role models.

It's Not Just Testosterone

Fathers have more to offer than an added measure of testosterone. When a father chooses to be a reliable figure in his son's life, it communicates to his son that he has someone to explore with, play with, talk with, and depend on to contribute to his healthy development.

It has been proven that kids, especially boys, are more likely to express emotion in a healthy way, develop a healthy attachment that leads to heightened self-esteem, and succeed academically when the father is present and reliable. Researchers have found that these positive consequences continue into the child's adulthood as they begin to enter the workforce.

The role of a father or positive male role model is not just vital for children but also for the mother of those children. When only the mother is available, her life becomes consumed with caring for the children. This added stress can lead to unhealthy parenting practices and burnout. By having both parents present or someone available to call, these roles can be better established while still allowing the child to work on individual strengths and ambitions.

When Dad Can't Be Found

Research has found that when a father is not present, it is likely: The infant will be born preterm or with low birth weight.

The mother's stress is increased due to trying to fill the role of both "mom" and "dad." Many of these families will be low-income households. Children may struggle with regulating emotions, leading to increased aggressive behavior and difficulty with social skills. A child may become involved in risky behavior. Daughters may explore sexual promiscuity at an earlier age. Sons have the potential to struggle with gender identity and role confusion.

Even if the biological father role is filled by another, some of these figures become temporary or have the potential of being abusive. Children will be left with feelings of blame or emptiness as to why their father left.

Where Did He Go?

What is the reason these fathers are not staying around? For many, it is because they themselves were never given the opportunity to be loved and taught by their fathers what true fatherly responsibility and commitment looks like. The generational curse of taking the easy way out has become the norm in many communities.

While we must be careful not to make excuses for these men, many leave because of their inability to provide for their families, it is so sad but true. Not being able to do so leads an untaught man to turning and running away from their responsibilities. Unemployment and lack of education can also be contributing factors as to why fathers leave. When men feel they are not meeting the social and economic demands that define fathers, the idea of achieving other fatherly responsibilities decreases, and it may seem easier for them to run. Other reasons for father absence can include imprisonment, long work schedules, living location, even abuse within the home.

Steps To Helping Children of Absent Fathers

Though the negative consequences of father absence can be disheartening, there is still plenty of hope for these children.

Include positive extended male family figures in the child's life. Children can form strong relationships when they have a safe, positive, and stable male figure to rely on as they grow up. This could come from a grandparent, uncle, or another positive male family member. When these men are present for monumental moments in life, as well as day-to-day interactions, a void can be filled, and the child's confidence can grow. Including extended family can also provide other resources like helping to reduce stress overload and the feelings of loneliness that mom may be dealing with.

If there, is no male family member available or near to help, try finding a mentor in your community. When a child is able to spend time with a successful individual in their community, different doors of potential are opened to them to see ways that they can become successful. Examples of mentors could be coaches and teachers.

Find support groups in the local area. Just as children can find mentors, single mothers can find others working through these same difficulties. There truly is strength in numbers. Brainstorm, network, and help each other. Though we may not be able to change the past, the future trajectory can be a positive one. Make time for yourself.

Growing up without a father brings risks and many challenges, but that does not mean it is the end, and it does not determine you or your child's future. Fatherless families can become resilient in their circumstances if the child's guardian is willing to do the necessary work.

It is also important that you let those who interact with your child know about their struggles. Teachers, caretakers, and other community figures can help alleviate the difficulties your child may face. But they cannot help if they are not aware. Remember, there is hope for brighter tomorrows.

We must also remember that there are fathers who choose to stay in their child's life after growing up without their father. Though these men may seem few in comparison to the work before us, it needs to be said that there are still positive male role models out there doing everything they can to instill godly ways and knowledge into our boys. You do not have to let the absentee determine what your family will become.

Poverty

I agree with Kierre Rimmer, the founder of F.L.Y. (Forever Lifting Youth), a program based in Cleveland, MS. He says that Mississippi's African American boys are more likely to live in poverty than children in all other racial and ethnic groups. Feel free to see where the African American boys in your community and State stand.

Black boys in Mississippi are consistently performing worse on national reading and math standardized tests than other groups. Black males are twice as likely to be unemployed in Mississippi. These are a few of the findings of two new reports from the Hope Policy Institute that examine education and economic security gaps of black males in Mississippi. The saying goes, if you are planning on going somewhere you must first know where you are. I encourage you to look at the stats in your communities and States and ask yourself how, how is such a brilliant people in this shape and then ask yourself what YOU PLAN ON DOING ABOUT IT.

Reports have concluded that "creating opportunities for young men and boys of color to reach their full potential helps to advance individual opportunity, family sustainability, community prosperity, and a state's overall economic competitiveness." In other words, given the immense challenges that African American males face, policies that help them could also help that state start climbing off the bottom of any number of lists where the state ranks low for citizens' quality of life, according to people who work with black boys and teens.

Connecting kids to business owners, professionals, and other community leaders, as well as teaching basic life skills like how to change a flat tire can change the mindset of a boy. I have lived by this rule for a why now and I have seen the difference that it has made in so many young lives.

It is important to introduce young people to the concept of entrepreneurship, especially our young boys because they are feeling the pressures of unfunded homes. The pressure to have money at 13 or 14 should not be a focus for kids, it should be the parents' responsibility. Kids should be enjoying life at 13 or 14 without worrying about where the money is coming from. Kierre says, generally, white kids don't have this problem.

Natalie Collier, the director of The Lighthouse | Black Girl Projects in Jackson, MS works with young women of color in the South. She also agrees that there is an expectation for black kids to grow into adulthood quickly. She believes, as I do, that this can be harmful to black families.

When the man is not present in the home, we do a disturbing and discrediting thing to our boys by telling them that they are now the men of the house, no they are still children. We place on them the responsibility to do a job that they are not prepared to do, many times setting them up for failure in the future.

We don't let girls be girls and boys be boys. We don't let them be children. The Hope Report illuminates those pressures. It shows that while Mississippi has the highest-in-the-nation poverty rate, 18.70 percent, more than 30 percent of Mississippi's black males are poor compared to about 10 percent of white men in Mississippi. Of all minority groups in poverty, black boys show to be the largest group affected in my state. Where do they stand in yours?

The Hope Institute shows that poverty plays a major role in shaping the health, education, and long-term outcomes of Mississippi's black men and black youth. The stress of poverty can also affect the psychological health of individuals and families. Molly Bashay and Corey Wiggins, reporters for the Hope Institute, claim that black men living in states like Mississippi are much more likely to encounter the negative effects of poverty and live in communities that are similarly affected by entrenched generational poverty.

Cassio Batteast, a director for a leadership institute for black boys in Jackson, MS, says that most of the boys he works with come from single-mother-headed households, and many of them feel pressure to contribute to the household's finances.

"A lot of them get in trouble because they are trying to help the family," Batteast says. "They are breaking into people's houses and doing other stuff just to help fill the gap that has been left by their fathers. Many find themselves behind bars in the process, and when kids are locked up in Juvenile Detention Centers, they can fall behind in school, making them more likely to drop out. If they are not old enough to drop out, most, if not embraced by a positive male role model, just hang around until they can."

From standardized test scores to high school completion to college remediation, Mississippi's black boys are lagging behind, according to another Hope report titled "Closing the Education Equity Gap for Mississippi's Black Males." It shows that the National Assessment of Educational Progress (NAEP) fourth through eighth grade reading and math scores for Mississippi black males are consistently lower than state and national averages. Advocates say we need to rethink policies that have disproportionate negative effects on black males.

Batteast, also says, "If we want to have safe, productive communities and society, it would be wise on our part to focus on the group that is having the most challenges. If we say these are the students that are having the most challenges, if we make sure they are successful, it automatically increases the districts and the state's success. In return, the poverty rate decreases, crime decreases, and the overall outlook on the community goes from negative to positive."

Jeremiah Smith, a former teacher who runs the Rosedale Freedom Project in Bolivar County, said schools should adopt what are known as restorative practices over zero-tolerance school discipline policies.

"For example, if two kids get into a fight at school, restorative practices would involve mediation with peers and support staff instead of calling the police and automatic suspension," Smith says. "This type of policy change would help the students as well as the overburdened and under-resourced school system. Stressed out administrators and teachers would have an easier job if they would do the hard work now to reconfigure discipline systems so that later they would not be putting out the same fires repeatedly."

Role Model Explained

What is a Role Model?

The words Role Model refer to an individual who takes out the time required and intentionally puts in the work to lead others through situations or life in general using his or her own life experiences and life lessons. Their goal is to not only encourage but also assist others in achieving.

Conclusion

The work to change and restore the lives of our young men in our communities today has become overwhelming. The need for positive male role models and fathers is greater now than ever before. The work remains plentiful, and the importance of the Positive Male Role Model is evident.

We, as Godly men, and Positive Male Role Models, must be willing to fight through whatever is taking place with our young men today. We must be willing to reclaim our young men from a society and culture that has taken hold of them. We must once again put on the shoes that were handed down to us by positive male role models and begin walking as the MEN we were created to be.

If we want strong, God-fearing men to marry our daughters, head their homes, if we want God-fearing men to head our communities and mold the future generations of boys in a way that pleases God, then the time is now for each of us, as men, to take a look in the mirror and ask ourselves where we can make a difference. Not only in a young man's life but what can we do within our own lives that may cause our young men to see that something in us that they can trust.

If we are not willing to sacrifice ourselves for the younger generation, then we will not only fail ourselves but also our families, our communities, our churches, and our young men.

It's time to put the old man away and take on the NEW MAN, the one that God calls His human foundation, His first.

We, as MEN, are the foundation. Let us pray for the strength, confidence, and wisdom of every MAN that steps out on faith today as he takes on the great challenge of being a Positive Male Role Model with the determination of saving our boys from self-destruction.

REFERENCE

- Center for Health Journalism. "Our Work Reporting: Impact of Absent Father on Mental Health of Black Boys." Retrieved from centerforhealthjournalism.org
- Forever Families. "Father Abandonment: The Consequences, Reasons, and Resilience." Retrieved from foreverfamilies.byu.edu
- Johnson, Rick. *Better Dads, Stronger Sons*. Grand Rapids, MI: Revell Publishing, 2006.
- MacArthur, John. *The MacArthur Study Bible NKJV*. Nashville, TN: Nelson Publishing, 1997.
- Mississippi Today. "Are Black Males the Key to Improving Mississippi?" Retrieved from mississippitoday.org
- Washington, Denzel. *A Hand To Guide Me*. Des Moines, IA: Meredith Publishing, 2006.

Made in the USA
Columbia, SC
06 November 2024